# ROLL UP YOUR SLEEVES

**STANDING UP
TO THE CHALLENGES OF LIFE**

# TUNDE JAIYEBO

Published in Nigeria by
J-Charis Media House
Cultural Centre road, Mokola,
G P O Box 15617 Dugbe,
Ibadan, Oyo State.

## FOREWORD

## FACING THE STORMS OF LIFE

"According to the Bureau of Standards in Washington, a dense fog covering seven city blocks to a depth of 100 feet is composed of less that one glass of water. That amount of water is divided into about 60 billion tiny droplets. Yet when those minute particles settle over a city or the countryside, they can almost blot out everything from your sight."

Many Christians today live their lives in a fog. They allow a cupful of troubles to cloud their vision and dampen their spirit. Anxiety, turmoil and defeat strangle their thoughts.

*Their lives are being "choked by the cares of this world"*
***(Luke 8; 14).***

*But "God has not given us a spirit of timidity, but of power and love and discipline"*
***(II Tim. 1:7).***

"Let's not let the fog get us down! Let's live in the Sunshine!" -The Paper Pulpit

Life, at various stages throws different dangerous darts at us – disappointment, distress, discouragement, disillusionment, etc and there is no way we can win in life using kids gloves. Life demands toughness, resilience and hard work. This book, ROLL UP YOUR SLEEVES, will aid you to face life headlong so that you can barge your way into success. You will learn how to handle, among other things, rejection, offences, discouragement, worry, limitation, guilt, low self- esteem etc

Why go through life weighed down by challenges when you can be a champion reigning and ruling in the affairs of life? Roll up your sleeves and get to work. You have just one life to live so make the most of it and enjoy it!

# Table of Content

# HANDLING REJECTION

Each of us has experienced rejection - times when, for no apparent reason, another person turned against us, did some things or made some remarks that made us feel and look like "a nobody". Rejection makes us feel unloved, unwanted, useless and insignificant. Rejection attacks the root of our self-esteem. Rejection creates a sense of unworthiness, a lack of self-acceptance, and inability to build healthy relationships. We feel unworthy and think others view us as the same way.

When we fail to accept ourselves, rejection has an open door to our emotions and this can have far reaching negative effects. If left unchecked, rejection will control our attitudes, actions, our relationship with other people and even with God. We cannot totally avoid rejection because we cannot control the way people feel about us. Some will like, appreciate and make us feel good. Others may reject us without reason.

## SYMPTOMS OF REJECTION

There are some identifiable symptoms in the life of a person that may point to the existence of rejection.

- Undue desire to please people;
- Inability to say "no" to people for fear of being rejected;
- Inability and unwillingness to reject people's demands so as to avoid hurting their feelings;
- Fear of other people's opinions;
- Undue desire to be noticed and acknowledged;
- Difficulty in trusting people;
- Perfectionism;
- Projecting a false sense of superiority;
- Overemphasis on one's weakness, inadequacies, faults and failures;

- Taking criticism personal;
- Critical spirit;
- Inferiority complex;
- Superiority complex;
- Resentment, bitterness and self-pity.

## A STITCH IN TIME SAVES NINE

Once we discover we have symptoms of rejection, we need to deal decisively with it. Undermining or delaying the treatment of the symptoms of rejection can be disastrous. A stitch in time, they say, saves nine. Dealing successfully with rejection requires honesty and a willingness to get to the root of the problem, which is a poor view of our self-worth. Every case of rejection attacks our perception of who we really are and if the foundation of our self-esteem is faulty, the feeling of rejection is inevitable. It is therefore, crucial that we have a proper and accurate perception of who we really are and the basis of our understanding must be right. When we understand who we are, then, we can properly place and handle other people's opinions of us. Our self-worth should never be based on the opinions of others, else, we are sure to suffer disappointment and rejection.

## UNIQUE ONE OF A KIND

We must understand we are unique, special and one of a kind. Out of the over six and a half billion people in the world, no one is a duplicate of another. We are all originals. There is nobody like you - so you are incomparable and public opinion does not and cannot change that fact. If adverse opinion about us is correct then, honesty, humility and common sense demands that we admit our shortcomings, adjust, make amends and move on.

> *"If you listen to constructive criticism, you will be at home among the wise. If you reject criticism, you only harm yourself; but if you listen to correction, you grow in understanding."*
> **Proverbs 15:31, 32** *New Living Translation*

*"Valid criticism is as treasured by the one who heeds it as jewelry made from finest gold."*
**Proverbs 25:12** New Living Translation

We must never feel threatened by what people feel or say about us, especially if it's false. Usually, people who criticize maliciously are people who don't engage in any progressive activities. The earlier we understood that everybody has a right to express his/her opinion, the better for us. We will then be able to tolerate and handle public opinions without feeling rejected.

## WHO DO YOU THINK YOU ARE?

The root cause of rejection is being unsure of our identity. We cannot afford to have an identity crisis. When we don't know who we really are, we automatically put a limit over our lives and unduly expose ourselves to be wounded through rejection.

When we know who we are, we automatically have an in-built mechanism to shield us from rejection. Knowing who we are gives us confidence and makes us unstoppable. Since we know who we are, whatever people say, do or think cannot make us feel small. We don't feel insulted by the opinions of men and we don't crave for the accolades of men. We know our self-worth is not the product of people's opinions.

Knowing who we are will help and deliver us from being defined by what we do or don't do. We are not what the environment defines us to be or what people define us to be. Who we are is not a function of what we do or what people think. If our identity is based on people's opinion, then we are in for a lot of trouble because people's opinion is at best fickle. The opinion of people is like the wave of the sea – it vacillates between high and low. Those who shout "hosanna" today, will cry "crucify him" tomorrow. Those who celebrate us today might discard us. Cathy Lechner in her book "If I'm God's Handiwork, Would Someone Please Explain These Thighs" made this great illustration about people –

"The greatest thing about the ministry is the people. The worst thing about the ministry is the people. People are like elevators. They'll take you up when you do something they like, or they'll take you down when you disappoint them."

## YOUR TRUE IDENTITY

If we are to successfully handle rejection, we cannot go through life riding on the identity we have acquired from the opinions of people. Our true identity is found only in God. He is the only authentic source to define our identity. We are who God says we are. He is our creator and He is the best authority to define who we are. Walking in the reality of what and who the bible says we are is the best cure for rejection. The identity God has given us in His word is the final authority and the only true basis to define our identity. Here are a few of how the bible describes us:

- Fearfully and wonderfully made;
- Apple of His eyes;
- Salt of the earth;
- Light of the world;
- Chosen generation;
- Peculiar people;
- His workmanship;
- Royal priesthood;

Handling rejection demands that we keep looking up, studying, meditating, confessing and living in the light of what and who God says we are. We must never forget that we are who God says we are and we can do what He says we can do. Any opinion contrary to God's opinion about us must be discarded no matter the source.

## BEWARE OF THE VACILLATION

There are three major sources of opinion about us — people's opinions, our own opinion and God's opinion. Our attitude, reaction and response to each of these three sources determines how far we go and how rejection affects us. Handling public opinion is crucial to dealing with rejection. As long as we are in this world, we cannot completely run away from public opinion – what other people will say about us and about what we do. If we do nothing, we get castigated for being indolent and if we make impact with our lives, we stand the risk of being criticized. The truth about life is that we cannot please everybody. In life, we please some and we displease others but life goes on. The Lord Jesus Christ made an interesting remark in **Matthew 11:16 – 19** (New Living Translation).

> *"How shall I describe this generation? These people are like a group of children playing a game in the public square. They complain to their friends, 'We played wedding songs, and you weren't happy, so we played funeral songs, but you weren't sad.' For John the Baptist didn't drink wine and he often fasted, and you say, 'He's demon possessed.' And I, the Son of Man, feast and drink, and you say, 'He's a glutton and a drunkard, and a friend of the worst sort of sinners!' But wisdom is shown to be right by what results from it."*

The moment we make up our mind and begin to fulfill our purpose, we automatically spark off reactions. People will begin to take a closer look at us and our work. Professional observers and commentators will have a new assignment. We become their next assignment and the object of commentary. The pursuit of any worthwhile dream will always put the "dream executioner" on a high pedestal that makes him susceptible to adverse public opinion. With the decay, darkness, decadence and seemingly hopelessness of our society, (where dog eats dog), our desire to stand out and be different will no doubt make tongues wag. To be radically different from others will attract attention – queries will be raised, questions will be asked and if we are not sure of ourselves and who we are, we will cave in and choose the common path of the ordinary. An inaccurate perception of who we are will get us swallowed up in the quagmire.

## STONES, TREES AND FRUITS

Public opinion can be adverse or complimentary. Nobody likes adverse publicity but if we are going to make any impact with our lives, adversity and adverse publicity are integral parts of life. We can either decide to feel rejected by adverse public opinion or we can choose to respond to it appropriately and continue the pursuit of our dreams. There is a saying that stones are only thrown at trees with ripe fruits. When we become the target and object of mudslinging, then we should know we are making good progress; enough to attract attention. The major reason why people feel rejected or react negatively to public opinion is insecurity and a low or faulty self-esteem.

When our self-esteem is based on what people say, we successfully set ourselves up for rejection. We must never allow false public opinion to make us feel inferior, inadequate or resentful. We have to keep our cool and keep our focus because public opinion can be very dangerous as it has the capacity to distract us from our assignment. We must never succumb to the temptation to answer armchair critics as it is just a waste precious time, emotions and resources.

# BARRIERS AND LIMITATIONS

Life indeed is not a bed of roses. We cannot stroll through life leisurely and expect to have our dreams realized. Life is a challenge that must be taken on headlong. Life is designed for men and women, who will take the bull by the horn, face life and give life whatever it takes to succeed. In life, things don't happen by accident. Life is not for weaklings.

"The biggest club in the world is the down-and-out club. Most men are brittle. They are like a pitcher that goes in to the well, hits a stone and is broken in pieces. Most men start out in life gaily until they hit a stone. Then they are done for. They might do well in a world that is filled with cushions but they are of little value in a world filled with stones." H.N. Casson

To live successfully in this life, we need to acquire skills in handling some inevitable challenges that will rear their ugly heads against us. Life is full of barriers and the man who will make anything out of life must learn to overcome every barrier that comes his way.

## LIMITATIONS

Many people have had their dreams and visions terminated, hindered or destroyed due to the limitations imposed on them by barriers and difficulties.

Limitations are conditions, factors or circumstances that get us incapacitated. Instead of being enabled, we are disabled and we are denied the ability to do what needs to be done. We cannot rise above a particular point or level.

Being limited can be a very frustrating experience. We have a deep yearning to advance, we know we ought to make progress but we are contained. We are like a bird trapped and caged.

## WHY PEOPLE ARE LIMITED

People can be limited in accomplishing their vision by many factors. Let us look at some reasons why people find themselves limited.

## 1. ENVIRONMENTAL FACTORS

Some are limited because of the environment - the economy may be depressed, the political situation may be unstable and if things were better, they probably would be able to accomplish more. The truth of the matter is that there is hardly ever a perfect timing or condition.

*"If you wait for perfect conditions, you will never get anything done."*
### Ecclesiastes 11:4
*New Living Translation*

Rather than wait endlessly for that perfect condition, we can still make the best of whatever situation we find ourselves. Our environment needs not limit us.

## 2. ANCESTRY

Some are limited by their ancestry. They think that they are from the "wrong" family. They have an inferiority complex and a self-imposed prejudice which militates against them in whatever they do, especially if it has to do with relationships. Such people usually excuse their limitation by blaming it on the system which does not favour people like them. This is a fallacy which we must not give in to.

## 3. OPINIONS OF PEOPLE

Some are limited by the opinions of others about them. People think and tell them they cannot make it, so they believe the lies. A man in the Bible who had such problem but was able to overcome it was Jabez. Due to the circumstances of his birth, his mother's opinion of him was negative. His mother even labeled him a man of sorrow.

*"And Jabez was more honourable than his brethren: and his mother called his name Jabez, saying Because I bare him with sorrow"*
**I Chronicles 4:9.**

Wherever Jabez went his name was against him. Jabez means "he will cause pain" or "man of sorrow". The reason why he was so called was due to the experience and opinion of his mother. Jabez realized he had a problem so he had to cry unto the Lord. He wanted a complete turnaround.

*"And Jabez called on the Lord God of Israel, saying, Oh that thou wouldest bless me indeed, and enlarge my coast, and that thine hand might be with me, and that thou wouldest keep me from evil, that it may not grieve me! And God granted him that which he requested."*
**I Chronicles 4:10**

A proper look at the above verse reveals that all Jabez wanted was the complete reversal of his situation. He no longer wanted to be identified with sorrow and pain. He wanted a change from the way his mother had painted him. He wanted to be blessed indeed and he wanted his coast enlarged. He wanted to rise above the limitation placed on him by the opinion of man.

If we are going to rise above limitation, we must have the attitude of Jabez. It is when we are intolerant of our present situation that we can experience change. Intolerance of the present creates the future. If we do what Jabez did, we will obtain similar results.

## 4. LOW SELF- ESTEEM

Others are limited by themselves. They think they are failures, never-do-wells and so they are limited. They have a low self-esteem. They don't see themselves the way that God sees them. They cannot see themselves succeeding. Others can make it but they cannot. They are like the Israelites mentioned in **Numbers 13:33.**

*"And there we saw the giants, the sons of Anak, which come of the giants and we were in our sight as grasshoppers, and so we were in their sight."*

The Israelites saw themselves as small. They had a poor perception of themselves – "and we were in our sight as grasshoppers". They did not see the greatness of their God. They had forgotten the great and mighty things God had done for them. They had forgotten the miracles of their deliverance from Egypt, the parting of the red sea, the provision of manna, meat, water etc. They put a limitation on themselves by "themselves" and consequently, they aborted the dream of entering the Promised Land. Out of the whole lot, only the two people (Caleb and Joshua), who saw themselves as God saw them, entered the Promised Land. The rest, apart from children below twenty-one years old, perished in the wilderness.

*"And Caleb stilled the people before Moses, and said, Let us go up at once, and possess it; for we are well able to overcome it."*
**Numbers 13.30.**

## 5. BAD EXPERIENCES / FAILURE

Many times mistakes of the past can limit people, and if care is not taken, such people lose confidence in themselves.

> **Frequent mistakes destroy our motivation and can create a barrier such that we are unable to seize opportunities that lie ahead**

It is not only a limiting factor but it also destroys our confidence. The devil uses our experience of frequent failures to taunt us with the fear of failing again and this limits the extent to which we can go. All this need not be. If we have failed in the past, we can still succeed today and have a bright future. God does not determine our future based on our past – our future is determined based on His plan and purposes which are encapsulated in His word (the bible).

*"For I know the plans I have for you," says the Lord. "They are plans for good and not for disaster, to give you a future and a hope."*
**Jeremiah 29:11.**

## 6. DEVILISH ROADBLOCKS

Limitations can also be roadblocks placed on our way by the devil to stop us from getting to the promised land of fulfilled dreams, desires and aspirations. The devil is always set to hinder us through all possible means whenever we set out to do God's will. He will mount his illegal roadblock just to slow us down or stop us entirely. We must be very sensitive to discern when the devil is at work. Limitation is not a respecter of persons. Every human being is susceptible to and open to limitation – the issue is to know how to identify and deal with it. We must understand that life is on three dimensions - human, demonic and divine. When we are not under divine influence, then we are under demonic influence and we cannot fight demonic influence with physical means.

## THE LIMITATIONS OF APOSTLE PAUL

The great Apostle Paul was faced with a demonic limitation in
**1 Thessalonians 2:17-18**

> *"But we, brethren, being taken from you for a short time in presence, not in heart, endeavoured the more abundantly to see your face with great desire. Wherefore we would have come unto you, even I Paul, once and again; but Satan hindered us."*

Notice the description of how Paul desired to see the Thessalonians – *"endeavoured the more abundantly to see your face with great desire"*.

His desire was intense, strong and fervent but he was still hindered from seeing his desire come to reality.

*"Wherefore we would have come . . . but Satan hindered us".*

All Paul had in return for his desire was regret – *"I would have come".* Many people have strong desires to get some things done - it could have been the desire to start a business, pursue a career, execute a dream project etc but, many times, the end result is usually summarized as "I would have but. . . "

Limitation is not a respecter of persons. Even the great apostle of faith, the great apostle who penned over two-thirds of the New Testament. . . even Paul who wrote in **Philippians 4:13** that

*"I can do all things through Christ which strengthens me"*

Despite his credentials and spiritual stature and status, he was limited and hindered.

*"Wherefore we would have come unto you, even I Paul, once and again; but Satan hindered us."*

Paul made several attempts but to no avail. Thank goodness, he knew the source of the problem.

*" . . even I Paul once and again but satan hindered me."*

The word "hinder" here means to "to cut into, to break up the road, to place an obstacle sharply in one's path". The devil can engineer limitations but thank God we have power over him and his works.

*"For whatsoever is born of God overcometh the world: and this is the victory that overcometh the world, even our faith."*
**I John 5:4.**

## HOW TO IDENTIFY LIMITATIONS

The following will help us to identify the operation of limitations in our lives:

## UNFINISHD TASKS

This is a clear manifestation of limitation. This can be caused by lack of proper planning, inadequate projection, laziness or sudden exhaustion of resources. The world is never sympathetic to people who abandon their ship mid-stream.

> *"For which one of you intending to build a tower, sitteth not down first, and counteth the cost, whether he hath sufficient to finish it? Lest haply, after he hath laid the foundation, and is not able to finish it, all that behold it begin to mock him saying this man began to build, and was not able to finish."*
> **Luke 14:28-30**

The man who had the dream to build the tower was limited and so became a laughing stock.

> *". . . all the spectators  start  to make fun of him"*
> **Luke 14.29b Moffat Translation.**

We need to realize that we are objects of observation both by human beings and by the "cloud of witnesses".

> *"Wherefore, seeing we also are compassed about with so great a cloud of witnesses, let us lay aside every weight, and the sin which doth so easily beset us, and let us run with patience the race that is set before us."*
> **Hebrews 12:1.**

The devil wants us to be disappointments. He wants us to end up as laughing stock. He wants us to be objects of mockery and shame. He is all out to ensure that we are limited and contained.

> **Limitation, usually, is the brain behind unfinished projects and the end result is, we stand the risk of being mocked, jeered at and made fun of.**

## MEDIOCRITY

Mediocrity also reveals the deadly work of limitation. Mediocrity is the "art of the middle road". It is doing things in a way that is neither very good nor very bad… "It's just okay, it's manageable". Mediocrity is doing the barely minimum. It's not stretching ourselves or going the extra mile. Mediocrity limits and cuts us off from excellence. If we do ordinary things, then our lives will be ordinary, but if we go the extra mile, our lives will stand out from the ordinary.

## LACK OF FULFILMENT

Lack of fulfillment in doing a certain task can cause limitations. Someone said, "If you hate your job you will soon begin to hate your life". A lack of fulfillment and deep inner satisfaction in whatever we spend our time doing will affect our life and can cause us to be limited.

## EXCUSES

We can identify a person plagued by the infirmity called limitation by the way he talks - he makes excuses for his failure, mediocrity or laziness. Such phrases as, "I cannot because . . ., It's impossible because . . . , It's difficult . . . , I was hindered/disturbed by . . ." are indications of the presence of limitations.

No matter the cause or the reason for limitation, the good news is that limitation can be overcome.

## THE SPIRIT OF LIMITATION

In some cases, a limitation can be a "demonic one". There is what is called the spirit of limitation. Until you are free from the hold of this spirit, you can labour and work hard till "kingdom come", you will always be limited.

# DESTROYING BARRIERS AND LIMITATIONS

The desire of the Lord is that we live above barriers and limitation. He wants us to be free to do all that He has planned for us. He wants us to be able to do

*"all things through Christ which strengthens you"*.
**Philippians 4:13.**

God wants us to flourish and fulfill His plan for our lives. The will of God is that we carry out to letter His vision, plan and purpose for our lives. We have been created to be a blessing to our generation. No matter where we are now, it's never too late to be on the road to making it. The dream God has put in us can still be translated into reality and we must be determined to destroy every barrier that might be a limitation to us. Where we are now is not where God is taking us, so we need to keep moving. We have God's backing to succeed and nothing should stand between us and what God has planned for us.

## BARRIER BREAKERS

*"So God created man in His own image, in the image of God created he him; male and female created he them, And God blessed them, and God said unto them, Be fruitful and multiply, and replenish the earth, and subdue it: and have dominion."*
**Genesis 1:27, 28**

Part of God's mandate for man was that he should subdue and have dominion. To subdue means to conquer, to subjugate, to tame. To have dominion means to control and have power over. If God told man to subdue and have dominion, it means that circumstances and situations will arise that could make man subdued and controlled. God therefore knows that in our sojourn on earth, limitations and barriers will come our way. He has therefore instructed us to deal with such situations. He will not ask us to do something we are not able to do.

> *"…his commandments are not grievous (hard to keep.)"*
> **I John 5:3b.**

> *"…the people that know their God shall be strong, and do exploits."*
> **Daniel 11:32b.**

## BORN TO DESTROY BARRIERS

We must understand we are divinely designed and equipped to be barrier breakers. An experiential knowledge of God gives strength - we are enabled and emboldened to do great things. We are energized to blast limitations off our way. The strength to do exploit can be ours as we take time out to know God. It is important that we decisively spend time in knowing God as this is a fundamental issue.

> *"Fear thou not; for I am with thee: be not dismayed; for I am thy God: I will strengthen thee; yea I will help thee: yea I will uphold thee with the right hand of my righteousness."*
> **Isaiah 41:10.**

God has the ability to do the seemingly impossible. He makes ways in the wilderness and rivers in the deserts. Where we think there is no more hope is exactly the point where God starts to do His own thing.

> *"For with God nothing shall be impossible"*
> **Luke 1:37.**

When we face seemingly impossible situations, we must remember we have a God with whom nothing is impossible. He is not bound by our limitation so He is our best adviser and helper. We are born of God and God has placed within us a mechanism and the wisdom to destroy barriers and overcome limitations.

*"For whatsoever is born of God overcometh the world: and this is the victory that overcometh the world even our faith."* **1 John 5:4.**

## NO QUICK FIXES

We need to search the word of God and find out by ourselves what God is saying about our situation. Search the scriptures, read, study, meditate and obey it. Once we let the word of God be a part and parcel of our life, we are on the road to overcoming limitations. The problem with many people is that they want a quick-fix. Quick-fix remedies work but they work only for a quick period – they never last. A foundation built on the word of God is bound to last for ever. Our relationship with God must be vibrant and ongoing.

## TALK IT OVER WITH GOD

When we foresee danger or even when we hit the wall, we should always go to God. We must avoid fretting or dabbling with worry.

*"Casting all your cares upon Him for He careth for you."*
**1 Peter 5:7.**

God cares for us. Let us see how other translations put the latter part of 1 Peter 5:7.

- He makes you His care;
- He takes care of you;
- You are His personal concern;
- His great interest is in you;
- He is concerned for you;
- He cares for you affectionately and cares about you watchfully.

We should always go to God, discuss with Him and seek His counsel. Whenever we are faced with a difficult situation, no matter how it might manifest itself, we need a word from the throne of grace.

*"If any of you lack wisdom, let him ask God, that giveth to all men liberally; and upbraided not; and it shall be give him."*
**James 1:5.**

When we seek His face, we must wait upon Him for His reaction. We must not just unload our worries upon Him, we must learn to be patient to wait for a reply and His direction. It is in the place of waiting that strength comes.

*"But they that wait upon the Lord shall renew their strength; they shall mount up with wings as eagles; they shall run, and not be weary; they shall walk and not faint."*
**Isaiah 40:31.**

Many times, we run into trouble because we refuse or neglect waiting upon God. We must cultivate the habit of waiting upon the Lord.

As we wait upon God in the place of prayer about the limitation, He will direct and show us the way out. We must be open to the leading of the Lord and be ready to be obedient. Obedience opens doors to God's blessings.

## DON'T GIVE THE DEVIL AN OPPORTUNITY

Many limitations are illegal roadblocks set up directly or indirectly by the devil to hinder the accomplishing of God's purpose.

> **We must always be on our guard so that whenever the ugly head of limitation is being reared, we put the devil in his proper place.**

Don't give him any opportunity at all.

*"Neither give place to the devil."*
**Ephesians 4:27.**

The devil is an outlaw - the moment we give him one inch he takes a mile, if we give one mile he takes ten. The way to frustrate the devil is by refusing to dwell on the problem.

If we dwell on the limitation, the devil will seize the opportunity to magnify it beyond what we can cope with. This is bound to get us discouraged to the point of giving up totally. We need to be like Abraham as stated in **Romans 4:18-21.**

> *"Who (Abraham) against hope believed in hope, that he might become the father of many nations according to that which was spoken so shall thy seed be. And being not weak in faith, he considered not his own body now dead, when he was about a hundred years old, neither yet the deadness of Sarah's womb: He staggered not at the promise of God through unbelief; but was strong in faith, giving glory to God; And being fully persuaded, that what he had promised, he was able to perform."*

The devil wants us to be unduly pre-occupied with limitation. He wants to keep our eyes off God by clouding our vision with impossibilities. The moment we do this, we give him the opportunity and room to operate. At this stage, our faith begins to weaken.

> *"And being not weak in faith he considered not His own body now dead, when he was about a hundred years old, neither yet the deadness of Sarah's Womb."*
> **Romans 4:19**

Abraham was definitely aware of his humanly impossible situation. Abraham however "considered not his own body." He refused to dwell on it or else, his faith would have been weak. Rather, he became "strong in faith, giving glory to God" (Romans. 4:20). We must stand against the wiles of the devil.

> *"Put on the whole armour of God that ye may be able to stand against the wiles of the devil."*
> **Ephesians 6:11.**

The devil operates through wiles. "Wiles" means cunning strategy and plan to deceive an enemy. The devil wants to deceive us especially by planting contrary thoughts into our mind. We need to stand against his plan and not give him any opportunity.

*"Casting down imaginations and every high thing that exalteth itself against the knowledge of God and bringing into captivity every thought to obedience of Christ."*
**2 Corinthians 10:5.**

We are to arrest every thought that wants to take our focus off God and His purpose for our life. We must ensure our thoughts are in obedience with and in compliance with God's word.

## DON'T SHUT UP

The words of a believer are very potent. Our words are backed up with divine power. As kings, our words are powerful.

*"And hath made us kings and priests unto God and his father."*
**Revelation 1:6a.**

When we speak, it passes as a king's word because we are kings and the words of a king are taken seriously.

*"Where the word of a king is, there is power."*
**Ecclesiastes 8:4a.**

We must be conscious of the power available in our words. When limitations stare us in the face, we must confront them by speaking God's word to them.

*"For verily I say unto you, that whosoever shall say unto this mountain, Be thou removed, and be thou cast into the sea; and shall not doubt in his heart, but shall believe that those things which he saith shall come to pass; he shall have whatever he saith."*
**Mark 11:23.**

Command the limitation to be removed and be replaced with God's provision. Speak God's word to your situation. Many of the miracles the Lord Jesus Christ performed were done by him speaking what He desired. He also cast out devils by His spoken word. He raised Lazarus by His spoken word. He healed the sick by His spoken word. He calmed the raging storm by His spoken word. The fig tree got dried up to its root by the spoken word. As we too begin to speak God's word to our situations, we will see results. Embedded in God's word is the ability and power to perform.

*"For as the rain cometh down, and the snow from heaven, and returneth not thither, but watereth the earth, and maketh it bring forth and bud, that it may give seed to the sower, and bread to the eater: So shall my word be that goeth forth out of my mouth: it shall not return unto me void, but it shall accomplish that which I please, and it shall prosper in the thing whereto I sent it."*
**Isaiah 55:10, 11.**

As we speak to the limiting factors militating against us, we must believe God expectantly for a change and it will surely come. Keep on speaking the word to the limiting situation and the situation has no choice but to bow at the end of the day.

The problem with many people is that they speak for a while and then quit. Remember quitters don't win and winners never quit - so keep speaking.

## A BIRD IN THE HAND IS WORTH TWO IN THE FOREST

Barriers and limitations tend to blind us and undermine whatever we have. In our bid to deal with barriers and limitations, we have to learn not to focus on what we don't have but on what we have. The question is not what we lack, but rather what do we have? A bird in the hand, they say, is worth two in the forest. What we have is much more precious, valuable and useful than what we don't have. Many people pray," Lord give me big faith so I will do great things"- this sounds like a very logical prayer, but in reality it is a clear evidence of unbelief. What have we done with our "mustard-seed faith" that we have now?

> *"…For verily I say unto you, if ye have faith as a grain of mustard seed, ye shall say unto this mountain, Remove hence to yonder place; and it shall remove: and nothing shall be impossible to you."*
> **Matthew. 17:20.**

We need to know that our promotion and our provision for the future depends greatly on how we handle the few things we have now.

> *"His Lord said unto him, Well done, thou good and faithful servant: thou hast been faithful over few things, I will make thee ruler over many things; enter thou into the joy of thy Lord."*
> **Mathew 25:21.**

## APPLY THE FORCE OF PATIENCE

We cannot leave patience out of the equation when dealing with limitations. True biblical patience is a force and not a passive, complacent wait. Patience is being consistent in holding on to God and His word despite the contrary situation around. Faith and patience work together.

> *"Then, knowing what lies ahead for you, you won't be bored with being a Christian, not become spiritually dull and indifferent, but you will be anxious to follow the example of those who receive all that God has promised them because of their strong faith and patience."*
> **Hebrews 6:12** *New Living Translation.*

As we believe God for a breakthrough, we must stick with Him come rain, come shine. Sticking with God and believing that He will do what He has promised is patience. Patience gives an assurance that it's going to be just as God has said. Patience is that persistent and tenacious hold on the integrity of God and

His word even in the midst of circumstances that are contrary. *"Cast not away therefore your confidence which hath a great recompense of reward. For you have need of patience, that, after ye have done the will of God, ye might receive the promise."* **Hebrews 10:35-36.**

# CASE STUDIES ON HANDLING BARRIERS AND LIMITATIONS

## CASE STUDY 1: FEEDING 5000

**Mark 6:35-44**

*"And when the day was far spent, his disciples came unto him, and said, this is a desert place, and now the time is far passed: Send them away, that they may go into the country round about, and into the villages, and buy themselves bread: for they have nothing to eat. He answered and said unto them, Give ye them to eat, and they said unto him, shall we go and buy two hundred penny worth of bread, and give them to eat? He saith unto them, how many loaves have ye? Go and see. And when they knew, they say, five and two fishes. And He commandeththem to make all sit down by companies upon the green grass.And they sat down in ranks, by hundreds and fifties. And whenHe had taken the five loaves and the two fishes, He looked upto heaven, and blessed, and brake the loaves and gave them toHis disciples to set before them; and the two fishes divided heamong them all. And they did all eat, and were filled. And theytook up twelve baskets full of the fragments, and of the fishes. And they that did eat of the loaves were about five thousandmen."*

In verse **35** we see two limiting factors:

- "The day was now far spent…"
- "This is a desert place…"

The disciples were faced with these two strong limitations to feeding the people. The limitations were genuine, legitimate and real.

## EXPOSE LIMITATION: DON'T DISGUISE IT WITH LEGITIMATE EXCUSE

No barrier or limitation is legitimate enough to stand between us and what God wants to do in our lives. Our dream is a gift from God so we must not allow anything to stop its execution. Genuineness of barriers and limitations are not enough reasons to allow limitations to ruin our vision. We should not allow any limitation to be disguised in the form of legitimate excuses.

*"The sluggard will not plow by reason of the cold; therefore shall he beg in harvest, and have nothing".*
**Proverbs 20:4.**

It is the lazy man that gives excuses; he puts his limitations in the sweet coat of legitimate excuses. "It is not easy to plow in the cold" - good excuse but such attitude will result in begging, lack and regret.

So the disciples had two very good excuses which made them react in verse 36.

"Send them away. That they may go into the country round about, and into the villages, and buy themselves bread: for they have nothing to eat".
Whenever we accept limitations we are on the road to making a compromise. The desire of the Lord was to do a miracle to feed the multitude but the disciples were ready to compromise this plan due to their wrong thinking in respect of the limitations.

## DON'T FOCUS ON WHAT YOU DON'T HAVE

The response of the Lord in verse 37 is very interesting. He told them, "… Give ye them to eat." Jesus was operating on a different wavelength entirely. He was telling them that "do not focus on what you don't have, but on what you have". He was saying the disciples had the capacity and ability to give the multitude food to eat.

When we are faced with an impossibility or a limitation, let us always realize that we can "give ye them to eat". The disciples in their shock resorted to Jesus and said "This is impossible and impracticable."

## INVESTIGATE WHAT YOU HAVE

The next two statements of Jesus are very vital and we must grasp the principles being enunciated.

"He said unto them, how many loaves have you? Go and see." Jesus was emphasizing his very first statement in verse 37 with his response in verse 38. He was saying, "don't focus on what you don't have but on what you have". He said, "how many loaves have you?"When we are faced with limitations we should always ask ourselves"what exactly do I have now?"

As long as we do not assess ourselves and find out what we have, the limits to fulfilling our vision will not be removed.

The disciples did not have any clue as to what they had. Jesus had to order the disciples to do something. He said "go and see", that is, they were ordered to "go and investigate". The latter part of verse 38 says, "and when they knew". They did not know until they had made an investigation.

Upon investigation, they discovered they had five loaves and two fishes. They realized they had something.

We will be surprised about what we have when we "go and see". When we realize what we have, we then have the materials to smash our limitation and receive a miracle. When Jesus knew what the disciples had, He began to make some moves.

## CALM THINGS DOWN

"And he commanded them to make all sit down by companies upon the green grass."

He commanded everybody to sit down. Why? Since it was late ("the day was now far spent" verse 35) and the people were obviously hungry and tired. There must have been some confusion. Some were already sleeping, some standing, some squatting, some babies were being comforted by their mothers, some groups of kids were running about etc.

Jesus had to <u>calm down</u> the situation. Everybody was to <u>sit down</u> on the <u>green grass</u>. You need to master the art of calming your environment down.

A confused and disorderly environment is never conducive to progress.

Jesus not only calmed the people down, he also told them to be organized.

*"And he commanded them to make all sit down by companies upon the green grass and they sat down in ranks, by hundreds, and by fifties,"*
**Verses 39 & 40.**

Preparation is the foundation for success. The crowd was to sit by "companies", in ranks of "hundreds and fifties". Preparation demands prayerfully making out a plan. Have a strategy. Look up to heaven for supply and multiplication. We must dedicate whatever we have to the Lord and then begin to make use of it in line with the plan set out.

## STEP OUT AND USE WHAT YOU HAVE

*"And when he had taken the five loaves and two fishes, he looked up to heaven, he blessed, and brake the loaves, and gave them to his disciples to set before them; and the two fishes divided he among them all."*
**Verse 41**

To fail to plan is to plan to fail. It is in the process of using what we have that multiplication occurs. We have to maximise what we have or else we will end up just managing the little we have.

*"Verily, verily, I say unto you, except a corn of wheat falls into the ground and die, it abideth alone…"*
**John 12:24a.**

We will be surprised to see how much we could achieve with the little we have.

*"And they did all eat and were filled."*
**Verse 42.**

Not only will we be fulfilled and be a blessing, but we will also have abundance.

"And they took up twelve baskets full of fragments, and of the fishes".

One vital reason for planning is to help us measure our effectiveness. Jesus planned and asked the people to sit down in the ranks of hundreds and fifties for many reasons such as:

- To allow for effective, even distribution of food to every rank.
- To enable a quick count of those fed.

## CASE STUDY 2:
## THE CASE OF PETER AND JOHN

*"Now Peter and John went up together into the temple in the hour of prayer, being the ninth hour. and a certain man lame from his mother's womb was carried, whom they laid daily at the gate of the temple which is called Beautiful, to ask alms of them that entered into the temple; Who seeing Peter and John about to go into the temple asked an alms. And Peter, fastening his eyes upon him with John, said, heed on us. And he gave heed unto them expecting to receive something of them. Then Peter said, Silver and gold have I none; but such as I have give I thee: in the name of Jesus Christ of Nazareth rise up and walk. And he took him by the right hand, and lifted him up and immediately his feet and ankle bones received strength. And he leaping up stood, and walked, and entered with them into the temple, walking, and leaping, and praising God. And all the people saw him walking and praising God: And they knew that it was he which sat for alms at the Beautiful gate of the temple: and they were filed with wonder and amazement at that which had happened to him."*
**Acts 3:1-10.**

Peter and John had to attend a prayer meeting and at the entrance of the temple was a lame man who asked them for alms. Unfortunately, Peter and John had no money on them; so, they were limited in helping the lame man. The most obvious option open to them was either to ignore the man's request, or tender an apology and move on. However, they did not focus on what they did not have. I am sure this particular incident was not their first encounter with the lame man. The man was a landmark at the temple. He was a point of reference at the Beautiful gate.

*"And a certain man lame from his mother's womb was carried, whom they laid daily at the gate of the temple which is called Beautiful, to ask alms of them that entered into the temple".*
**Verse 2.**
*Peter and John were men of prayer.*
*"Now Peter and John went up together into the temple at the hour of prayer, being the ninth hour of prayer."*
**Verse 1.**

They must have passed by the man many times, focusing on their inability to help him. But on this fateful day, they had a change of focus. They recognized what they did not have.

*"Then Peter said, Silver and gold I have none".*
**Verse 6a**

However, unlike other days, they knew they had something. They refused to focus on what they did not have but on what they had.

*"….but such as I have …"*
**Verse 6.**

They focused on what they had. Like the feeding of the five thousand, what they had became a spark to ignite the miracle. They used what they had.

*"…but such as I have give I thee; In the name of Jesus Christ of Nazareth, rise up and walk."*
**Verse 6.**

When we use what we have we receive strength for a miracle. *"And he took him by the right hand, lifted him up: and immediately his feet and ankle bones received strength. And he leaping up stood, and walked, and entered with them into the temple, walking and leaping, and praising God."*
**Verse 7, 8.**

Things are not really as bad as they look. Once we make up our mind to focus on the right things, then we are on the road to success. What are you passing through now? Are you plagued by limitations? Are your plans being threatened by limitations? The Lord wants us to rise above our present state to a higher ground. Go to God in prayer and as you prayerfully apply these principles, your expectation shall not be cut off. You cannot afford to be discouraged. The journey of life is still far- there is so much ground to cover, so much territory to conquer.

# HANDLING DISCOURAGEMENT

The world has never been a tougher place to live in. Things seem to get tougher and life seems rougher by the day. The economic climate is very gloomy. The political situation is chaotic. The social life has been very unsettling. Crime is on the increase, violence is the order of the day. The security of life and property can hardly be guaranteed. People are losing hope as the environment is not in any way conducive to realize one's dreams.

## LIVING IN THE SURVIVAL MODE

The major pre-occupation of a vast majority of people is just to simply survive and keep going. Most people just barely keep their head above water and they are just clinging to their dear lives. Life and people have dealt a great and bitter blow on them; that the courage to soar high and live their dreams has evaporated. The number of people living in the valley of discouragement is unusually high. Everywhere you turn, the song is the same – discouragement.

## IT'S TOO EXPENSIVE

Discouragement is a dart that will be thrown at us at different times in life but the issue is our response.

We cannot afford to let what is happening in and around us make us give up on our dreams – we cannot afford to be discouraged.

If we are to make the desired impact with our lives, we must learn to weather the storm and cross over every barrier that discouragement puts across our path.

## WHAT IS DISCOURAGEMENT?

Discouragement is derived from two words- dis and courage. 'Dis'- expresses negation. It indicates reversal or absence of an action or state. It indicates an expulsion from something. Therefore, the word discouragement means the absence or negation or expulsion of courage. Courage means the ability to disregard fear. It means bravery. When a person is said to be discouraged, it means he has lost or does not have the ability, strength, confidence or energy to do what ought to be done. It means the confidence to act has been deflated; there is no motivation or incentive to act.

## A SUBTLE DESTROYER

Discouragement creates a feeling of despair in the face of obstacles; it kills the desire and the drive to maneuver through the rough patches of life.

Discouragement is one of the most subtle and destructive tools to a man's success. Discouragement is a waster, a destroyer and a killer. Once discouragement sets in, it begins to make one's strength leak. Once strength begins to leak, the power to be consistent in the execution of one's dreams, goals and desires quickly ebbs away and the consequences of discouragement begins to set in.

Discouragement brings depression, inconsistency, anxiety, fear, stagnation and ultimately, the seemingly available option is to quit. Countless number of people have sacrificed their dreams and desires on the altar of discouragement. Discouragement kills initiative. Discouragement stifles creative thinking and makes the execution of ideas impossible. Discouragement steals the ability to persevere. Discouragement denies us the benefit of the satisfaction and fulfillment derived from accomplishment. We are robbed of the feeling of a job-well-done. Discouragement leads to abandoned projects. It destroys dreams. It kills visions. It leaves a trail of regret and wasted resources.

The incident in Ikings 19 gives us a very good case-study on the causes and solutions to discouragement.

*"And Ahab told Jezebel all that Elijah had done, and withal how he had slain all the prophets with the sword. Then Jezebel sent a messenger unto Elijah, saying, so let the gods do to me, and more also, if I make not thy life as the life of one of them by to morrow about this time. And when he saw that, he arose, and went for his life, and came to Beer-sheba, which belongeth to Judah, and left his servant there.*

*But he himself went a day's journey into the wilderness, and came and sat down under a juniper tree: and he requested for himself that he might die; and said, it is enough; now, O Lord, take away my life; for I am not better than my fathers. And as he lay and slept under a juniper tree, behold, then an angel touched him, and said unto him, arise and eat.  And he looked, and, behold, there was a cake baked on the coals, and a cruse of water at his head. And he did eat and drink, and laid him down again. And the angel of the Lord came again the second time, and touched him, and said, Arise and eat; because the journey is too great for thee. And he arose, and did eat and drink, and went in the strength of that meat forty days and forty nights unto Horeb the mount of God.*

*And he came thither unto a cave, and lodged there; and, behold, the word of the Lord came to him, and he said unto him, what doest thou here, Elijah?"*
**I Kings 19:1-9.**

*"And he said, 'I have been very jealous for the Lord God of hosts: because the children of Israel have forsaken thy covenant, thrown down thine altars, and slain thy prophets with the sword; and I, even I only, am left; and they seek my life, to take it away. And the Lord said unto him, Go, return on thy way to the wilderness of Damascus: and when thou comest, anoint Hazael to be king over Syria:"*
**I Kings 19:14-15.**

*"Yet I have left me seven thousand in Israel, all the knees which have not bowed unto Baal, and every mouth which hath not kissed him."*
**I Kings 19:18.**

Let us look at the principles and lessons we can glean from the experience of Elijah.

## CAUSES OF DISCOURAGEMENT

## I. NOT BEING APPRECIATED OR VALUED

*"And Ahab told Jezebel all that Elijah had done, and withal how he had slain all the prophets with the sword."*
**I Kings 19:1.**

As human beings, we have the tendency to get discouraged when we are not appreciated or adequately valued. With Elijah stamping out and wiping the land clean of devilish agents that were turning the heart of God's people from the true and living God, one would have expected him to become a national hero and probably an adviser to the government of the day, but he was neither recognized nor rewarded.

Whenever we think we are given a raw deal, it elicits the feeling that we have labored in vain. It's like one has sacrificed and strained oneself to no benefit. This leads to regret of one's actions.

The human nature craves for appreciation. We all want to be given a sense of belonging. We all want to have that feeling of "being wanted". When we are not appreciated and when we are treated as if we do not exist or matter, we feel disappointed. Disappointment eventually leads to depression and nonchalance; all of which are the by-products of discouragement. There is weariness and lack of desire to continue doing what ought to be done.

The way to avoid this tendency is to realize that God is the only one who can truly and properly appreciate, value and reward us. We must have a mindset that all we do is for the Lord and He is our "rewarder".

> *"Remember, the Lord will pay you for each good thing you do,*
> *whether you are slave or free."*
> **Ephesians 6:8** *The Living Bible.*
> *"For God is not unrighteous to forget your work and labour of*
> *love, which ye have shewed toward his name, in that ye have*
> *ministered to the saints, and do minister."*
> **Hebrews 6:10.**

> *"But without faith it is impossible to please him: for he that*
> *cometh to God must believe that He is, and that he is a*
> *rewarder of them that diligently seek him."*
> **Hebrews 11:6**

## 2. BAD LIGHT

When we are painted in a bad light, it has a knock-on effect on our attitude. It can discourage us. In verse1 of 1 Kings 19, we see Elijah being painted in a bad light. Bad light simply means we are misinterpreted and misrepresented. Of all the things that happened, it was only the killing of the prophets that was reported to Jezebel. Discouragement usually comes when we are misrepresented especially by people who we look up to. When people that we least expect misunderstand or misrepresent us, we get discouraged. Ahab did not remember the rain, neither was it recorded that he mentioned the fire from heaven that consumed the sacrifice, wood and water etc.

To avoid this we must be like Jesus.

> *"Your attitude should be the same that Christ Jesus had.*
> *Though he was God, he did not demand and cling to his rights*
> *as God. He made himself nothing; he took the humble position*
> *of a slave and appeared in human form. And in human form he*
> *obediently humbled himself even further by dying a criminal's*
> *death on a cross."*
> **Philippians 2:5 – 8** *New living Translation.*

## 3.  ADVERSITY

Discouragement also sets in when we are faced with adverse situations - this is especially made more serious if the adverse situation threatens our peace, joy, position or our life.

In Elijah's case, it was the fear of losing his life.

> *"And when he saw that, he arose, and went for his life, and came to Beer-sheba, which belongeth to Judah, and left his servant there."*
> **I Kings 19:3.**

> *We must not allow fear into our lives, as fear is not of God.*
> *"For God hath not given us the spirit of fear; but of power, and of love, and of a sound mind."*
> **2 Timothy 1:7.**

## 4. LOSING SIGHT OF GOD'S PROMISES

We become discouraged when we lose sight of God's promises – His love, mercy, provision, protection etc. Many times, the physical circumstances that we face can be so overwhelming that we get pressured to putting God off the scene. When Elijah saw the developments, his response was to throw in the towel and run. He shifted his gaze from the greatness of the God he was serving to the adversity and opposition facing him.

> *"And when he saw that, he arose, and went for his life, and came to Beer-sheba, which belongeth to Judah, and left his servant there."*
> **I Kings 19:3.**

Elijah had been used by God to do the seemingly impossible. He called fire down from heaven. Fire licked up water. He also ordered the killing of the 480 prophets of Baal.

Usually, after the mountain top experience comes the valley experience. Elijah was confronted by Jezebel's threat to his life and he was completely overtaken by it. The question to ask is "if he could have called fire down from heaven, why did he not first do a demonstration to put Jezebel in her place?" Discouragement makes us lose focus and paralyses us into inaction.

We all face this situation every once in a while. We have had great experiences, great landmark moments but we have all had times when our reaction completely deflates who we were at the other side of our exploits. Life many times is not a simple straight road - there are mountains, valleys, detours, obstacles, rivers, deserts, etc and success in life demands that we learn how to handle different terrains in which we find ourselves.

The key to this is to regularly meditate on the word of God - not just when things are bad but also when things are fine. We prepare for war in the time of peace. Care must be taken so that we don't get carried away by the good times, but take quality time out to equip ourselves for the future.

## 5. " I'VE HAD ENOUGH"

When people think they have had enough, the next bus-stop is discouragement.

> *"But he himself went a day's journey into the wilderness, and came and sat down under a juniper tree: and he requested for himself that he might die; and said, it is enough; now, O Lord, take away my life; for I am not better than my fathers."*
> **I Kings 19:4.**

## 6. WRONG SELF- CONCEPT

Wrong self-concept is an open door to discouragement. When we don't see anything good or special in ourselves or we think that we have lost everything special/unique, life will be tough and the courage to do anything will be difficult. Elijah said '…I am not better than my fathers' Verse 4.

Wrong self-concept, especially in hard times, will de- motivate us to press on in life. At such times we are more prone to discouragement. That is when we think such thoughts as 'If others who are better than me are finding it difficult, who am I to even try?'. The truth of the matter is that we are special and we must see ourselves like God sees us. We are who God says we are.

## 7. FEELING OF BEING ALONE

> *"And he said, 'I have been very jealous for the Lord God of hosts: because the children of Israel have forsaken thy covenant, thrown down thine altars, and slain thy prophets with the sword; and I, even I only, am left; and they seek my life, to take it away."*
> **I Kings 19:14.**

Whenever we have the feeling of being alone, it has the tendency to get us down. If we are involved in a team or a joint project and we discover or have the feeling that our colleagues or those with us are not forthcoming, we are bound to get discouraged. Our effort, our sacrifice, our labour will seem like a waste of time. It will look like we are wasting our resources.

In life, people are bound to abdicate or abscond from responsibility. The key to avoiding that from discouraging us, is never to be motivated by people's reaction or responses. There are times in life when we have to be lone rangers and trail blazers.

## 8. FEELIING OF BEING ABANDONED

> *"And he said, 'I have been very jealous for the Lord God of hosts: because the children of Israel have forsaken thy covenant, thrown down thine altars, and slain thy prophets with the sword; and I, even I only, am left; and they seek my life, to take it away."*
> **I Kings 19:14.**

We human beings live, thrive and survive on meaningful relationships and whenever we are deprived of such company, discouragement can set in.

The good part is that even when it seems that we are abandoned and left alone, there is someone who will never leave nor forsake us-God.

*"Let your conversation be without covetousness; and be content with such things as ye have: for he hath said, I will never leave thee, nor forsake thee."*
**Hebrews 13:5.**

## 9. SEVERE LOSS

Whenever we lose something or someone valuable, discouragement tends to set in. We wonder how on earth we can cope without what we have lost. We feel what we have lost is irreplaceable. At such times, we feel life can just not remain the same again.

## 10. DEPRESSION

The great prophet Elijah was bitten by the bug of depression. Depression is that state whereby a person is despondent, downcast and disheartened.

Depression brings sadness, despair, and discouragement. When depression steps in, these are some of the inevitable results:

- Low gloomy spirit;
- "Stand–offish" attitude;
- Loss of interest or pleasure in normal activities;
- Changes in sleep pattern;
- Changes in appetite;
- A deeply sad or depressed mood;
- Difficulty concentrating;
- Guilty feelings or feelings of worthlessness;
- Thoughts of suicide.

Nobody is totally immune from the attack of depression but it can be decisively dealt with.

## THE DEVIL'S PLOY

John Wesley in his famous sermon "Satan's Devices" states that satan has three main methods of discouraging the Christian:

- Damp your joy;

- Attack your peace;
- Target us especially in times of sickness and pain.

We therefore, need to watch out and never fall prey to the devil's ploy.

*"Lest Satan should get an advantage of us: for we are not ignorant of his devices."*
**2 Corinthians 2:11.**

## THE WAY OUT OF DISCOURAGEMENT

*"And as he lay and slept under a juniper tree, behold, then an angel touched him, and said unto him, arise and eat. And he looked, and, behold, there was a cake baked on the coals, and a cruse of water at his head. And he did eat and drink, and laid him down again. And the angel of the Lord came again the second time, and touched him, and said, Arise and eat; because the journey is too great for thee. And he arose, and did eat and drink, and went in the strength of that meat forty days and forty nights unto Horeb the mount of God."*
**I Kings 19:5-8.**

Despair, depression and discouragement are facts of life and we have a responsibility of handling them.

God told Elijah "Arise, eat and rest." Beloved, this is not the time to stumble and fall under the yoke of discouragement. The journey of life is still far so we need to buckle up, brace up, and badge our way forward. The journey of destiny is too great an issue to give up, so we cannot afford to be weak or depressed.

*"And he came thither unto a cave, and lodged there; and, behold, the word of the Lord came to him, and he said unto him, what doest thou here, Elijah?"*
**I Kings 19:9.**

## GET OUT OF THE VALLEY

To get out of the valley of discouragement, we will need to find out how we got into it. We need to do a proper and thorough diagnosis of our situation/problem. This can only be done by thinking and consulting with God in the place of prayers. We can do this by answering such questions as:

•What is the exact issue at stake? We will need to find out exactly what the problem is and not just the symptoms or the after-effect;

•What alternative course of action do I have? What options do I have to take to resolve the problem?

•Are there other issues/facts I need to lay my hands on so as to resolve the issue at hand?

## PRAYERS

The most fundamental factor in coming out of discouragement is to pray and trust God for help and deliverance.

> *"Save me, O God, for the waters have come up to my neck. I sink in the miry depths, where there is no foothold. I have come into the deep waters; the floods engulf me."*
> **Psalm 69:1-2.**

> *"Cast all your anxiety on him because he cares for you."*
> **I Peter 5:7.**

> *"I have told you these things, so that in me you may have peace. In this world you will have trouble. But take heart! I have overcome the world."*
> **John 16:33.**

## THINGS ARE NOT AS BAD AS THEY LOOK

One funny thing about life is that bad times are not as bad as they look. With all the complaints of Elijah, God's response was that things were not as bad as he was painting them to be.

> *"Yet I have left me seven thousand in Israel, all the knees which have not bowed unto Baal, and every mouth which hath not kissed him."*
> **I Kings 19:18.**

Buckle up, things are not as bad as they seem.

Beloved, whatever you are going through now is not as bad as they look. You are not the only one going through what you are going through. You are not the first and you will not be the last to go through it. Whatever you are going through is not unique to you so don't let the devil isolate you.

> *"Give all your worries and cares to God, for he cares about you. Stay alert! Watch out for your great enemy, the devil. He prowls around like a roaring lion, looking for someone to devour. Stand firm against him, and be strong in your faith. Remember that your Christian brothers and sisters all over the world are going through the same kind of suffering you are."*
>
> **I Peter 5:7 – 9.**

# PULLING DOWN STRONGHOLDS

Success in life demands we have a balanced and accurate view of things. There are some behind-the-scene dealings going on that we need to be aware of. Life is not just natural or physical, but the spiritual has a crucial and usually unseen role. We must never make the mistake of looking at the outward appearance of things only. We must look at life with the eye of the spirit.

*"Do you look on things after the outward appearance?"*
**2 Corithians 10:7.**

Beloved, the devil has his agenda/plans for us and we cannot afford to be ignorant, careless or complacent.

*"Lest Satan should get an advantage of us: for we are not*
*ignorant of his devices."*
**2 Corinthians 2:11**

Ignorance is deadly and dangerous. We have an enemy out there who is all out to defeat, disgrace, derail and delay us; and one of his strategies is the use of strongholds.

## SLAVES, PRISONERS AND THE VICIOUS CYCLE

A stronghold is anything that has a strong hold on us; strongholds arrest and imprison us making us feel that it is impossible to make progress. At such times, we get frustrated by our inability to make a headway in spite of all concerted efforts.

Strongholds hold us down and make us slaves. Strongholds entrap and imprison us in a way that we cannot do what we ought to do. It is as though we are caged in and incapacitated. Strongholds make our lives go round in circles. Strongholds are the direct and indirect manifestation of the works of the devil. Strongholds are usually entrenched in our lives through thoughts, deception, wrong mindsets and repetitive bad experiences. A stronghold is anything that has held us bound despite several attempts to be free from it. Anything that has a strong hold on us is a stronghold. Strongholds get entrenched in our lives in many forms. They enter our lives through many doors. Inability to break free from grief, guilt and painful experiences can translate to strongholds. Inability to stop thinking evil, immoral and unprintable thoughts is also evidence of being under a stronghold.

Until we stamp our foot down, resist the devil and enforce our victory and freedom in Christ, we will be under the strangle hold of strongholds. Most cases of strongholds are the handiwork of the devil and there are many guidelines/instructions in God's word that deals with how to handle the devil and his manifestations.

## NO NEGOTIATION, NO DEAL

Nowhere in the Bible are we told to negotiate, tolerate or compromise with the devil. We are only told to deal decisively with him

> *"Be sober, be vigilant; because your adversary the devil, as a roaring lion, walketh about, seeking whom he may devour: Whom resist steadfast in the faith, knowing that the same afflictions are accomplished in your brethren that are in the wo rld."*
> **I Peter 5:8-9.**

Let's look at the implication of this powerful statement by Apostle Paul.

• Be sober – This means we have to be cool-headed, clear-minded, and in control. We must not be agitated, we must not fret neither must we panic. We must know that God does not respond to panic, anxiety, fretting or agitation. He responds to faith and His word.

• Be vigilant – We have to be alert. Our eyes must be open. We have to be watchful. We need to be vigilant because we have an adversary (one who is against us and is an antagonist to our interest)- the devil.

It is very important that we understand that the devil is not omnipresent – he cannot be present in two places at the same time. Only God is omnipresent. Due to this limitation of the devil, he operates through a network of agents. Hence the need for us to be vigilant so that we can recognize and resist his agents.

Paul describes the devil as "a roaring lion". Usually the roar of a lion is his instrument of intimidation. His roar instills fear and scares the daylight out of his impending prey. We must be on the lookout not to be intimidated by the devil or by whatever he orchestrates against us. The devil is desperate and on the prowl. Paul says the devil is "seeking whom he may devour" – he is looking for, and he is on the lookout for susceptible people to prey on. This is why we must be sober and vigilant. Our response and responsibilities in dealing with the devil are stated from verse nine.

*"Whom resist steadfast in the faith."*

The person to resist is the devil. He has to be resisted because he is our adversary. He is against us and our interest. The devil is all out to complicate matters for us. He is resolute, determined and unwavering in his pursuit; so we must resist him steadfastly. Our resistance must be persistent, on-going and relentless. There is no room to negotiate with the devil – he has to be resisted each and every time he rears his ugly head. When we do this in faith, the devil always responds by fleeing in terror.

*"Submit yourselves therefore to God. Resist the devil, and he will flee from you."*
**James 4:7.**

## FIGHT WITH THE RIGHT ATTITUDE

When we are under the yoke of strongholds, our attitude is very important. Like it is commonly said, attitude determines altitude. If we go through life with a wrong or faulty attitude, we are setting ourselves up for serious trouble.

We must avoid the natural tendency to think that we are the only ones who go through seemingly "irresolvable" problems. When we are faced with hard times or difficulties, we must never be deceived to think that everybody else is just having life easy and we are the only ones stuck; going through "the fire". We should not let the devil isolate us. We must be aware that we are not the first to go through such fiery times and we are surely not going to be the last.

*"Knowing this that the same afflictions are accomplished in your brethren that are in the world"*
**I Peter 5:9.**

Somebody someplace, somewhere, somehow is going through whatever we might be going through. Everybody is fighting one battle or the other.

Our attitude should also be that the battle has already been won. We are not fighting to win, we have already won.

*"Nay, in all these things we are more than conquerors through him that loved us."*
**Romans 8:37.**

We are asserting our victory. We are declaring our victory over defeated foe or enemy.

*"For whatsoever is born of God overcometh the world: and this is the victory that overcometh the world, even our faith."*
**I John 5:4.**

We must see strongholds as trespass – it is an illegal invasion of our lives which must be decisively dealt with.

Our third attitude should be one of being informed. Ignorance is deadly. The devil is a master in taking advantage of people who are ignorant.

> *"Lest Satan should get an advantage of us: for we are not ignorant of his devices."*
> **2 Corinthians 2:11.**

Ignorance is deadly when fighting any battle. In pulling down strongholds, we must have as much information as possible. We must know exactly who we are fighting against, our weapons and how to use them. We must know the God we are serving and our strategies must be worked out in conjunction with Him.

> *". . . But the people who know their God shall be strong and do great things."*
> **Daniel 11:32b.**

> *"For though we walk in the flesh, we do not war after the flesh: For the weapons of our warfare are not carnal, but mighty through God to the pulling down of strong holds"*
> **2 Corinthians 10:3-4.**

We must never fail to realize that though we are mortal human beings, we cannot use human weapons or strategies to fight our battles.

As Christians, we must realize that we have the advantage of being adequately equipped to deal with the affairs of life. We have access to the resources of God to pull down strongholds.

> *"Our weapons are mighty through God to the pulling down of strongholds."*
> **Verse 4.**

We, therefore, need to be aware of and maximize these mighty weapons.

## OUR WEAPONS

As Christians, we are equipped and endowed with great weapons such as:

### 1. The name of Jesus

*"Wherefore God also hath highly exalted him, and given him a name which is above every name: That at the name of Jesus every knee should bow, of things in heaven, and things in earth, and things under the earth; And that every tongue should confess that Jesus Christ is Lord, to the glory of God the Father."*
**Philippians 2:9-11.**

### 2. The word of God

*"For the word of God is quick, and powerful, and sharper than any two-edged sword, piercing even to the dividing asunder of soul and spirit, and of the joints and marrow, and is a discerner of the thoughts and intents of the heart."*
**Hebrews 4:12.**

*"Is not my word like as a fire? saith the Lord; and like a hammer that breaketh the rock in pieces?"*
**Jeremiah 23:29.**

### 3. Praises.

God inhabits the praises of His people and no devil dare operate in the environment where God reigns.

*"But thou art holy, O thou that inhabitest the praises of Israel."*
**Psalm 22:3.**

*"When mine enemies are turned back, they shall fall and perish at thy presence."*
**Psalm 9:3.**

A classic example in the case of praise as a weapon is that of King Jehoshaphat:

*"And when he (King Jehoshaphat) had consulted with the people, he appointed singers unto the Lord, and that should praise the beauty of holiness, as they went out before the army, and to say, Praise the Lord; for his mercy endureth for ever.  And when they began to sing and to praise, the Lord set ambushments against the children of Ammon, Moab, and mount Seir, which were come against Judah; and they were smitten. For the children of Ammon and Moab stood up against the inhabitants of mount Seir, utterly to slay and destroy them: and when they had made an end of the inhabitants of Seir, every one helped to destroy another. And when Judah came toward the watch tower in the wilderness, they looked unto the multitude, and, behold, they were dead bodies fallen to the earth, and none escaped. And when Jehoshaphat and his people came to take away the spoil of them, they found among them in abundance both riches with the dead bodies, and precious jewels, which they stripped off for themselves, more than they could carry away: and they were three days in gathering of the spoil, it was so much."*
**2 Chronicles 20:21-25.**

## 4. The blood of Jesus
*"We overcome by the blood of the lamb and the word of our testimony."* **Revelations 12:11.**

These weapons are available for us to use to pull down whatever wrong concept, idea or thought that is holding us captive. Identify the stronghold and pull it down in the name of Jesus. Pull down the stronghold of grief, guilt, sorrow, bad habits, immorality and inferiority complex in the name of Jesus and praise Him for your victory and freedom.

# HANDLING OFFENCES

We human beings, are classified as social beings and cannot do without meaningful relationships. Companionship is a fundamental factor in sustaining our wellbeing. Life is a web of relationships, and many times it is not without problems.

Offence is as a major hindrance to fruitful and continued relationship.

## SKANDALON

One of the major Greek words for offence is "Skandalon". Skandalon is the name of the part to which a bait is attached in a trap - it is the trap itself.

Skandalon is usually used metaphorically of anything that arouses prejudice or displeasure against people, groups or organizations. The words arouse and prejudice are very important.

Arouse – means to begin, create, originate or stir into action.

Prejudice – means an irrational attitude of hostility directed against an individual, group or organization.

An offence arouses prejudice. Offence causes anger, agitation and annoyance. It leads to bitterness and bias. When we are offended, we get upset, unhappy, dejected, rejected and disappointed. It makes us feel abused and cheated.

## WATCH OUT! IT'S A TRAP

Offence is a trap. Offence is a trap that hinders us from relating well with people. It stifles our relationship with people such that we do not get along with people with whom we used to have a good relationship with; causing disharmony and disaffection among groups. This means that when offences show up, pleasure takes its exit. Prejudice is a destroyer of joy. When we are offended, there is reversal/withdrawal of pleasure we earlier had in our relationship with the individual, group or organization before the offence. It destroys friendships. Offence is a tool in the hands of the devil used to destroy strategic relationships. He uses offence to disconnect and distract us from people, groups and organizations that have been set up and designed for our good. Offences hurt; wound our conscience; it breaks our heart and destroys confidence; It damages trust; pollutes the mind and it introduces negative bias and prejudice. To make any head-way in life, we must learn to handle offences. The Lord Jesus Christ made an interesting statement in **Luke 17:1.**

> *"Then said he unto the disciples, It is impossible but that offences will come: but woe unto him, through whom they come!"*

This means it is guaranteed, it is sure, certain and inevitable that we will all encounter offences at one time or the other. No matter what we do or don't do; no matter how we perform or don't perform, offences will come - Jesus said so. If offences are bound to come, then common sense dictates that we should prepare and arm ourselves to handle it. Beloved, it is not when offences come that we begin to run helter-skelter trying to salvage the situation – we prepare and get ready before it strikes. We prepare for war in time of peace. Since Jesus said offences are bound to come, the first step in handling offence is not to be surprised or shocked when it shows up. If we understand this, we will not make  statements as: 'I thought he was a pastor', 'I thought he was a Christian', 'I thought leaders are not expected to behave like that', 'I thought we were close friends' and other statements to such effect. When offences don't shock us, we can clearly deal with it. Offences are bound to come and they can come from any source and from anybody. We must understand that every man has a free will which he can use as he wishes. God has given every man the power of choice and freewill. If people decide to use their power of choice and freewill to offend us, we should not be shocked but rather see it as one of those things which we must handle.

## WALK IN LOVE

One of the surest guarantees against offence is walking in love. We must make up our minds to walk in love – agape love. When we walk in agape love - the God kind of love that loves in spite and despite anything, we are not likely to stumble when offences come.

*"Love never gives up, never loses faith, is always hopeful, and endures through every circumstance."*
**I Corinthians 13: 7** *New Living Translation.*

Love believes the best of people; Love always makes excuses for people's actions and in-actions. Love would say 'If only he knew, he would not have...'
Agape love is not necessarily a feeling but primarily a decision – an act of the will. We decide to walk in love no matter how we feel.

## EXAMINATION TIME

When offences come, our response or reaction to it reveals a lot of things. It provides us with an opportunity to examine ourselves. When we are offended, our weak points, many times, are revealed. Our vulnerable points are exposed. Many times our reaction to offences can reveal that we are too sensitive, edgy, touchy or irritable; it can show if we are spineless, unable to handle pressure and unfair criticisms. It reveals that we have the tendency to give up easily. Many times, offences exposes our abilities to write people off and give up on them. It shows the strength of our tolerance. It shows whether we can really endure hard times.

*"If thou faint in the day of adversity, thy strength is small."*
**Proverbs 24:10.**

When we get offended, we therefore, need to look inward to

examine ourselves. If we are going to have great influence on people, we cannot afford to be weighed down by offences as they are distractions. The only way to avoid distraction is to be prepared. Love makes allowances for people's faults and it forgives upfront. Forgiveness is a virtue that we cannot afford not to cultivate – be quick to forgive. Forgiveness, like love, is not necessarily a feeling but primarily a decision of the will. When we are quick to forgive, offence will not have an inroad into our lives. Forgiveness and forbearance are indispensable tools needed to keep offence out.

> *"Put on therefore, as the elect of God, holy and beloved, bowels of mercies, kindness, humbleness of mind, meekness, longsuffering; forbearing one another, and forgiving one another, if any man have a quarrel against any: even as Christ forgave you, so also do ye."*
> **Colossians 3:12-13.**

## BE ALERT!

In addition to being well informed about how and why offences come, we must also be aware that it can be a tool in the hand of the devil to destroy God-ordained relationships. We must realize that the devil wants us to get trapped in the Skandalon – he wants us to stumble and perish, so we need to be vigilant and take precaution.

> *"Be sober, be vigilant; because your adversary the devil, as a roaring lion, walketh about, seeking whom he may devour."*
> **I Peter 5:8.**

# CHAPTER EIGHT

# HANDLING WORRY

One of the greatest disservices we can do to ourselves is worry. Worry is feeling troubled, anxious or disturbed by actual or potential difficulties, without bringing any solution to the table. When we worry, we are bothered, perturbed and disturbed. Worry wears us out.

## WORRY IS A THIEF

Worry robs us of peace of mind. Worry denies us of the strength and creative ability to work our way out of difficulty. Worry destabilizes our thinking process – we just can't seem to see the woods from the trees. Worry makes us vulnerable to emotional distress, sickness, fear and unhappiness. Worry steals our joy. A worried man is uptight, uneasy and cannot relax.

## WRONG QUESTIONS

Worry makes us ask "what if", which leads to a lot other imaginary scenarios which compound our worries. Worry makes us uneasy as it navigates our mind more towards the negative rather than the positive. When we worry, we tend to see, focus and devote more attention to "the worse scene scenario" than on the "best scene scenario".

## THE ROCKING CHAIR

Worry is an exercise in futility and an ill wind that does nobody any good. Someone said that "worry is like a rocking chair – it gives you something to do but it doesn't get you anywhere".

A research study shows that eighty-five per cent of what we worry about never happens.

The origin and development of the word is very illustrative and helpful. Reader's Digest Word Power Dictionary comments on worry as follows:

"Worry was an old English word meaning 'strangle'. In Middle English it took on the meaning 'choke with a mouthful of food', 'seize by the throat and tear', and 'swallow greedily', and in the 16th century 'harass with repeated aggression'. This gave rise to 'annoy or disturb' in the late 17th century and 'cause anxiety to' in the early 19th century. The sense 'feel anxious or troubled' . . . is not recorded until the end of the 19th century."

Beloved, when next you are tempted to worry, know what you are getting yourself into. Worry looks at the options and anticipates the worst scene scenario; which then leads us to a state of panic, anxiety and fear. Worry makes us give undue credence and attention to negativity thereby robbing us of the joy, peace and certainty of the present. When worry sets in, it automatically chases peace of mind, optimism and enthusiasm away. Worry strangles our mind of constructive and creative thinking. Worry never produces any good fruit. Worry is a destroyer that pulls one down.

*"Worry weighs a person down"*
**Proverbs 12:25a** *New Living translation.*

Worry makes a simple problem look very difficult. Worry makes a difficult problem look complex. Worry makes a complex problem look impossible. Worry makes life unbearable. "Worry gives a small thing a big shadow". Swedish proverb.

## THE THREE COUSINS

Worry, anxiety and stress are three cousins which do no good. When we give room to worry, anxiety sets in and we get stressed. The three cousins are destined and determined to affect our health, relationships and life negatively if we don't checkmate them.

Worry is a serious distracting force which we need to decisively deal with. Worry makes us panic and make wrong judgments. The good news, however, is that worry can be dealt with.

## LAUGH AND LIVE LONGER

One very good medicine for anxiety and stress is laughter.

> *"A merry heart doeth good like a medicine: but a broken spirit drieth the bones."*
> **Proverbs 17:22.**

When we learn not to worry we lengthen our life.

> *"A relaxed attitude lengthens life"*
> **Proverbs 14:30a** *New Living Translation.*

We cannot live in denial of the uncertainty and adversity of the times but our only hope of survival is not worry, but God.

## CAREFREE LIVING

> *"Don't worry about anything; instead, pray about everything. Tell God what you need, and thank him for all he has done. If you do this, you will experience God's peace, which is far more wonderful than the human mind can understand. His peace will guard your hearts and minds as you live in Christ Jesus. And now, dear brothers and sisters, let me say one more thing as I close this letter. Fix your thoughts on what is true and honorable and right. Think about things that are pure and lovely and admirable. Think about things that are excellent and worthy of praise."*
> **Philippians 4:6-8** *New Living Translation.*

> *"Let him have all your worries and cares, for he is always thinking about you and watching everything that concerns you"*
> **I Peter 5:7.**

We must never succumb to the temptation that we have a right to hold on to our worries. We must that ensure we don't yield to the tendency to brood over, ruminate and dwell on our worries. We must never allow worry to dominate our minds, else we become enslaved to worry. We must learn to "cast all our worries on the Lord". So we can live a "carefree life".

Casting our cares upon God means that we trust Him to sort us out. The truth of the matter is that our worrying cannot yield anything positive.

*"Can all your worries add a single moment to your life? Of course not. "And why worry about your clothes? Look at the lilies and how they grow. They don't work or make their clothing, yet Solomon in all his glory was not dressed as beautifully as they are."*
**Matthew 6:27-29** *New Living Translation.*

## NO PITY PARTY, PLEASE!

Casting our cares upon the Lord, does not absolve us of the responsibility to specifically identify the cause and result of all our worries. We need to find out exactly what we are worried about and prayerfully find ways to resolve them. One great medicine for worry is sharing the problem with a trusted person who is competent to help us find a way out. A problem shared, they say, is a problem half solved.

Our sharing the source, object and result of our worry must be done with the right motive. We must never share our worries to get sympathy. We must never share our worries with people who will only throw a pity party for us. We must never share our worries with people who cannot help us. We must only share our problems with people who are competent and courageous to help us.

Imagine a life devoid of worry and anxiety – what a life that will be! We must aspire to have such a life.

# HANDLING GUILT

When life deals bad blows on us, it affects every aspect of our lives. The fatal blows of life can leave an indelible mark, not just on our past, but also our present and future. For most people, when they get hit by the wrong side of life, they put their thinking caps on and they begin to hit themselves on the head for "finding" themselves in such predicaments. For most people they go on a guilt trip which ultimately leads to a depression. Guilt is the feeling we get when we take responsibility for the adverse situation or circumstances that have befallen us. Guilt is the outworking of our conscience that makes us "feel bad" for having fallen short of an expected standard. There is a right way and a wrong way to deal with guilt and hiding our guilt is not the solution.

## POSITIVE AND NEGATIVE GUILT

Guilt can be both negative and positive depending on our attitude and response to it. For us to truly and genuinely repent of any negative activity, we will need to acknowledge our wrong, feel guilty about it and be willing to make amends. Guilt is God's way of telling us that we have fallen short of His standard. Agreeing with God's standard is the right way to free us of guilt. Guilt, therefore, points us to God and makes us reconcile with Him and His standard.

## DESTRUCTIVE GUILT

Many times, guilt can be negative and destructive. Guilt can eat us up to the point that we lose the zeal, energy and motivation to pick up the pieces and move on with our lives. Guilt has the tendency to make us feel worthless. Guilt can be a serious immobilizer – it can make us cave in, withdraw and throw in the towel and just accept "our lot".

Guilt comes with her cousins – remorse, regret and depression. We just feel that life is not worth living. What used to give us joy and satisfaction will be meaningless and burdensome. The motivation for life and for living will be at the lowest ebb. Life will just look meaningless and worthless.

## IT IS A BLINDFOLD

Guilt can deny and rob us of the power and motivation to forget about yesterday and pursue tomorrow. It can blind us from seeing that there is light at the end of the tunnel, that a bright tomorrow is right ahead of us. When we are overwhelmed by guilt, we begin to feel that we have a problem or we are the problem. This robs us of the joy of living. The company of our loved ones and those who can help us become meaningless. A wrong approach to guilt will always blind us from leaving our past. It will deny us the power to move into the desired future that God has in mind for us.

## THE WAY OUT

Guilt is too heavy a burden to carry – we need help. We must come to God in confession and ask for His help.

> *"My guilt overwhelms me - it is a burden too heavy to bear."*
> **Psalm 38:4** *New Living Translation.*

> *"Come unto me, all ye that labour and are heavy laden, and I will give you rest."*
> **Matthew 11:28.**

The ultimate and surest solution to guilt is God. We need to go to God and pour our hearts to Him.

> *"Then I let it all out; I said, "I'll make a clean breast of my failures to God." Suddenly the pressure was gone - my guilt dissolved, my sin disappeared."*
> **Psalm 32:5** *The Message.*

## PULL YOURSELF TOGETHER

To come out of guilt, we will need to pull ourselves together so we can see the wood from the trees. We must come to the point where we realize that being emotionally down will not do us any good. We will need to find out exactly what the problem is to avoid chasing shadows. We need to be honest about the whole situation and avoid going into denial. We must face our fears and ask ourselves honest questions. What exactly is the problem? What options are there to solve the problem? What specifically has to be done to resolve the issues on ground? If we cannot find the way out of guilt by ourselves, then we need to seek external help.

## RENEW YOUR MIND

Guilt is a stubborn stain in our minds that is very difficult to remove, but we can solve this problem through the

*washing of the water by the word"*
**(Ephesians 5:26).**

We need to take time to renew our mind by interacting with the word of God. We must believe what God says about us.

*"So now there is no condemnation for those who belong to Christ Jesus."*
**Romans 8:1.**

This will demand we must make a U-turn from the way the world thinks to the way God thinks. Since guilt is a product of our thinking process, the way to deal with it is to deal with our mind. The only way to do this is to spend quality time reading, studying, hearing, meditating and doing what the bible says. Spending time in the word of God gradually "deletes" the wrong data in our mind and replaces it with the correct one.

*"Don't copy the behavior and customs of this world, but let God transform you into a new person by changing the way you think. Then you will know what God wants you to do, and you will know how good and pleasing and perfect his will really is."*
**Romans 12:2** New Living Translation.

# HANDLING INSECURITY

One of the root causes of problems in our society is insecurity. Far too many people are insecure so they need to prove that they have worth and value. An insecure person does not know who he really is. He feels unsafe and lacks confidence. He thinks what he does determines who he is, so he feels insulted when asked to do things "below him". An insecure person finds it difficult when asked to step down from a position. He will do everything and anything to remain in position of authority and power.

## SHOW OFF

Insecure people think that their status or position determines who they are so they can flaunt their position, power and possessions. They make a boast of whatever they have. They parade themselves in a way that they can be seen and given recognition. They try to draw attention and crave for credit when someone else seems to do a better job. When someone else does a better job or has better qualifications they feel threatened. An insecure person never hesitates to use threats and intimidation to have his way.

## THE SECURE PERSON

A secure person, on the other hand, knows who he is. He is not anxious to impress and makes no parade of himself or his achievements. He knows that he is not defined by what he knows or what he does. A secure person promotes and seeks the good of others. It is a joy to be around him – he makes you feel welcome. He removes every feeling of intimidation and he wants you to aspire to the top. A secure person takes criticism in good light. He is open-minded and open to new ideas.

## HEALTHY SELF-ESTEEM

To succeed in life, as we ought to, we must have a healthy self-esteem. Self-esteem is the basis of our being and our identity. It is the essence and substance of who we are. If our self-esteem is not built on the right foundation, it will collapse when it matters most. When our self-esteem emanates from material things - money, popularity, possessions or from status, position, association, name or education, we stand the risk of it crashing when these things are adversely affected. When anybody comes against these things or undermines them, our self-esteem is at risk. This is why some people will do virtually anything to keep their wealth, position, status and fame.

We must be careful not to build our self-esteem and self-worth on external things. What we have, what we drive or where we live is a risky basis to determine our identity and self-esteem. These external things are subject to change, destruction and depreciation. To therefore base our self-worth and identity on these things means when they go down, we go down too. External things are subject to the value society places on them and societal values are at best fickle. When society determines our self-esteem, we subject our lives to the whims and caprices of the system of the world. A time will come when we will not be able to meet up with the demands and standards that the society expects and nothing depletes and depreciates our self- esteem as much as not measuring up. A person whose self–esteem is based on people's opinion will be an emotionally imbalanced-person because people's opinion are never constant. Those that cry "Hosanna" today will shout "crucify him" tomorrow. Public opinion should not be a determinant of our person and identity.

## EVIDENCE OF LOW SELF-ESTEEM:

- Undue attention to people's opinion;
- Indecision and indecisiveness;
- Being unduly intimidated and having undue fear of people (their status, opinion etc);
- Fear of making mistakes;

- Fear of success;
- Undue desire  to please people;
- Taking criticisms personal;
- Making judgments based on comparison;
- Not wanting to hurt people (usually evidenced by the inability to say 'no' which leads to making unnecessary sacrifices).

To have a healthy self-esteem, we must realize that like every other human being, we have been made significant by God. Whatever anybody thinks, believes, says or does, does not change who we are. We are who God says we are. Our self-worth must therefore, be premised and based on the word of God which gives us the true picture of our usefulness and value. No one is more important than the other. Each one of us has his or her own unique God-given assignment and each person is the best man for the job - any other person is at best; the second best. When we understand this, we will face life with a positive attitude. A person with a healthy self-esteem will never be in competitive jealousy. He is in his own class and he has no time for the rat race. Someone said "whoever wins or loses in a rat race is still a rat".

# PERSONAL CHECK-UP

Charles Kettering, the inventor, had a unique method of solving problems. He would break down each problem into the smallest possible sub problems. Then he did research to find out which sub problems had already been solved. He often found that what looked like a huge problem had previously been 98 percent solved by others. Then he tackled what was left." Source: Unknown If we are to make the desired impact with our lives, we need to take regular time off to assess ourselves.

## DO YOURSELF A FAVOUR

Creating time for regular self-analysis is one of the greatest favours we can do ourselves. A person who does not take time to regularly examine himself stands the risk of ending up in a bad shape. We need to regularly take time out to ask ourselves questions such as:

- What am I doing now?
- What am I supposed to be doing?
- Where am I going with my life, my career, my family?
- Where am I supposed to be going?
- What is my vision?
- What is my dream?
- Where am I now in view of what my dream and vision demands?
- Where am I coming from and am I headed in the right direction?

We need to do periodic self-analysis, regular monitoring tests and evaluation exercises. This is crucial, so that we can know how close we are moving towards our dream and destiny. It helps us to monitor our progress rates and effectiveness. It will let us know if we are making progress relative to the maximal utilization of the resources that have come our way. The result of our self-analysis should propel us to roll up our sleeves and march on to victory in life. It will also reveal the problems, hindrances and obstacles militating against the successful execution of our dreams. It will help us know the things we are up against.

When we honestly ask ourselves these questions, it leads us to a conclusion which Paul also came to in **Philippians 3:13.**

> *"Brethren, I count not myself to have apprehended: but this one thing I do, forgetting those things which are behind, and reaching forth unto those things which are before."*

Notice the words "I count". Paul did a personal assessment. He did not wait for anybody to assess him. This is the mark of a person who is taking his life seriously; we should not wait for people to assess us before we notice our state.

Paul assessed himself and came to the conclusion that he had not yet arrived. The simple question to ask is, can there be arrival without a destination? Also, there can be no arrival without a departure. Do you have a desired destination in life? Do you have a defined goal or are you just drifting through life? Are you just "taking life as it comes" or you are taking the bull by the horn?

Beloved, we need to live strategically, regularly checking our progress in the journey of life.

> *"Brethren, I count not myself to have apprehended".*

Many times self-analysis will lead to the conclusion that we have not arrived, and if care is not taken, this conclusion can be very destructive. Notice Apostle Paul did not end his self-analysis here with the conclusion of not having arrived.

*"Brethren, I count not myself to have apprehended but…"*

## IT'S NOT THE END OF THE STORY

Where we are now is not the end of the story, there is still a "but". There are still many chapters to the book of our life. That word "but" is very crucial.

- You might not have arrived but…
- You might be missing it now but…
- You might be without a job now but…
- You might not have enough now but…
- Things might look gloomy now but . . .

No matter the conclusion of your self-analysis, there is still much more to be done. "But" implies that it is not yet the end of the story - so don't throw in the towel. There are at least three things to be done when we reach a conclusion after our self- analysis.

*"Brethren, I count not myself to have apprehended" but this one thing I do"*

The natural tendency when things are not working, when we see we have not made as much progress as we ought to is to panic. At such times we fret, get confused, get upset and begin to doubt our ability and our capacity to deliver. At such times there is the tendency to get distracted. Apostle Paul knew what to do so he said… "but this one thing I do", He knew he had to focus.

Focus keeps us steady, stable and standing on our two feet with our eyes fixed on the set target. Focus eliminates confusion and helps us to make the right choice.

*"Keep your eyes straight ahead; ignore all sideshow distractions. Watch your step, and the road will stretch out smooth before you."*
**Proverbs 4:25-26** *The Message.*

The second thing we need to do after we conclude our self-analysis is "forgetting those things which are behind". For us to move forward, we must have a right perspective of yesterday as we cannot move forward and look back at the same time. We cannot dwell on yesterday and expect to enter into a glorious future.

## THANK GOD YESTERDAY ENDED LAST NIGHT!

Yesterday is a powerful force; it is a very strong current that has a tendency to sweep its victim off its feet. Yesterday is a very crucial issue that has to be well handled else, it will mar today and mess up tomorrow. If yesterday was bad, it will haunt and taunt. A bad yesterday is all out to discourage us, it is determined to rob us of the courage needed to face today. Yesterday is a reminder - "can things really be the same again?" Yesterday sings loud in our ears "once bitten twice shy". A bad yesterday can be like a dark shadow that follows us wherever we go.

On the other hand, if yesterday was good, we have a desire to live in it. A good yesterday will want us to relish in the past, despise the present and invariably ignore the future. A good yesterday has the tendency to drag us into nostalgia – it wants us to be sentimentally attached to it at the expense of the future. It has a strong pull of wanting us to see things from the eye of the "good old days". A good yesterday kills the desire for adventure. It frustrates the creativity to try new things and it stifles the imagination.

Yesterday can be dangerous whether it is good or bad, so, we must learn to put yesterday where it belongs. We must understand and appreciate the fact that yesterday ended last night. If yesterday was bad, don't be scared to own up - face it and move on. Analyze what went wrong and make concrete plans not to repeat the mistakes of yesterday.

If yesterday was good-celebrate, build on its successes but still move on. Never build a permanent dwelling place on yesterday's success. Yesterday's excellence is today's mediocrity, so move on. Yesterday is gone and gone for ever.

Yesterday ended last night and thank God it did. Thank God yesterday ended last night as its demise gives the opportunity of a brand new day.

## YESTERDAY DIED LAST NIGHT

The death of yesterday affords the privilege of opening a new chapter of our history. We have lost yesterday and all we have is today which will also end soon. Today is the only guarantee that we have, so, we have to maximize all the opportunities that come our way today. Tomorrow is a privilege which we might not be offered, so, we have no choice but to learn from the mistakes of yesterday and build on the successes of yesterday. Yesterday ended last night so wake up to a brand new day.

*"Remember ye not the former things, neither consider the things of old. Behold, I will do a new thing; now it shall spring forth; shall ye not know it? I will even make a way in the wilderness, and rivers in the desert."*
**Isaiah 43:18-19.**

## MEMORY AND IMAGINATION

Two words are very important in the above passage: remember and consider. Both are located in the realm of the mind and of thoughts. To remember means - having or being able to bring to one's mind; to recall or recollect.

Consider means - to think carefully about; to take into account when making a judgment.

The big question is "are our thoughts based on yesterday?" If we are going to fulfill destiny and make indelible marks on the sands of time, we must learn to be free from yesterday.

We need to know the difference between memory and imagination. Memory replays the past while imagination "pre-plays" the future. Beloved, undue emphasis on yesterday will blind us from seeing our future. Isaiah 43:19 is a continuation of the thought in verse 18 and it starts with a powerful word "behold".

*"Behold, I will do a new thing; now it shall spring forth; shall ye notknow it? I will even make a way in the wilderness, and rivers in the*

*desert."*

Behold means see or look. If we don't do away with giving undue attention and emphasis to yesterday by remembering and considering it, we will not be able to see what is promised in Verse 19.

We must learn to put our past and our present situation in proper perspective.

We need to see the wood from the trees. A glorious and better tomorrow awaits us.

*"Behold I will do a new thing ..."*
**Verse 19"**

As long as we put yesterday in perspective, as long as we are expectant about what God will do we are in for a surprise. That glorious plan will "spring forth" when we least expect. To the surprise of every one, God shows up even when they have given up on us. The Lord also said He will even make "a way in the wilderness and rivers in the desert". This talks of the extra-mile dimension of God's love and promise for us.

## STEP OUT AND REACH FORTH

The third thing we can learn from Paul's experience is "reaching forth unto those things which are before". This talks of a constructive and persistent pursuit of a goal.

Notice 3 sets of words:

1. Reaching forth implies a stretching, an effort;
2. Those things deal with specifics and  not generalities and
3. "Which are before"- talks of the future.

What specific things are we reaching for? What specific goals are we pursuing? What specific targets are before us? Do we have goals and aspirations that put the stretch in us?

When we have no aspirations, goals or challenges there is nothing to live for. There is more to our lives than meets the eye. There is a vast amount of territory waiting for us to conquer. We cannot afford to let what we are going through and what we have gone through destroy what we have set before us. It is time to roll up our sleeves and face life squarely.

## FINAL WORD

The greatest and only sure source of victory in life is God. He is our power source and the only way we can be "plugged into" God is to make Jesus Christ our personal Lord and Saviour. This is the only authentic guarantee of getting great results when we roll up our sleeves to face life's challenges. To do this, say this simple prayer.

"Father, I come to you in the Name of the Lord Jesus Christ. I realise that I am a sinner. I believe in my heart and I confess with my mouth that the Lord Jesus Christ died for my sins. He was buried and on the third day, He was raised from the dead for my justification. I confess Him as my Lord and Saviour. Lord Jesus, come into my heart, be my Lord and Saviour. Father, I thank you that I am born again in Jesus Name. Amen."

# Other Books from J-Charis Media House

- Maximizing your Leadership Potentials
- No Way Mr. Devil
- Your Life Counts
- Thank God, Yesterday Ended Last Night
- A Fool's Profile
- Lazybones And What They Do
- Angry People And What They Do
- Proud People And What They Do
- Help! My Prayers Are Not Working
- Thank God For Potiphar's Wife
- Forgiveness101
- Guilt
- Moving Forward Through Diligence
- Use or Miss It
- Worry
- Rejection
- Offence
- Intimate expressions
- Leadership Handbook
- Principle of the seed
- Leadership Manual
- Leadership Matters
- Effective Leadership
- A – Z of Effective Ministry